Leaders of the Middle East

Blane Conklin, Ph.D.

Publishing Credits

Historical Consultants
Jeff Burke, M.Ed
Fernando Pérez, M.A.Ed.

Editors
Wendy Conklin, M.A.
Torrey Maloof

Editorial Director
Emily R. Smith, M.A.Ed.

Editor-in-Chief
Sharon Coan, M.S.Ed.

Creative Director
Lee Aucoin

Illustration Manager
Timothy J. Bradley

Publisher
Rachelle Cracchiolo, M.S.Ed.

Teacher Created Materials
5301 Oceanus Drive
Huntington Beach, CA 92649-1030
http://www.tcmpub.com

ISBN 978-0-7439-0675-3

Table of Contents

Meet the Leaders from the Middle East

Some of the world's most-known leaders come from the Middle East. Many of these leaders disagree with each other. This leads to **conflict**.

There are some leaders who are angry about Israel (IZ-ree-uhl). They do not think this nation deserves to exist in their region. Leaders from Egypt and Palestine (PAL-uh-stine) have reached out to make peace with Israel. Others have not been able to agree on peace treaties.

A few leaders promote **religious extremism** (ik-STREEM-izuhm). They let their religious beliefs excuse violence. These leaders want to see other countries ruled by an extreme form of Islam (is-LAWM).

In today's world, oil is a very powerful resource. The land in the Middle East has 65 percent of the world's oil. Everyone wants to control that oil. One leader from Iraq (ih-RAWK) was Sadaam Hussein (suh-DAHM hoo-SAYN). He started a war over oil.

Some of the leaders in the Middle East have made these conflicts worse. Others have tried to end these conflicts. It is because of these leaders and the issues they face that people focus on the Middle East.

Where Is the Middle East?

The Middle East is in the middle of the Eastern Hemisphere. Egypt and Turkey are the border on the west side of the Middle East. Pakistan is the border in the east. All the nations in between these countries make up the Middle East. Some of these nations are Syria (SEAR-ee-uh), Lebanon (LEB-uh-nuhn); Israel, Jordan, Iraq, Saudi Arabia, and Iran (ih-RAN).

This man sits by his desert tent in Saudi Arabia. There is an oil well behind him.

Early Egyptian Leader

Around 1500 B.C., a young woman named Hatshepsut (hat-SHEP-soot) lived in Egypt. Her young husband was the pharaoh (FAIR-oh), but Hatshepsut was the real power behind the throne. She made all the important decisions for the country. After a few years, people began to follow her orders. She then declared herself pharaoh. For 22 years, Hatshepsut worked to improve Egypt.

Connecting Two Seas

The Mediterranean (med-uh-tuhr-RAY-nee-uhn) Sea and the Red Sea are only separated by a small amount of land. A canal was built to connect the seas. It is called the Suez (SOO-ez) Canal. This is an important shortcut for ships in the area.

Can you locate the Suez Canal on this map?

There is a large ship coming through the Suez Canal behind this ferry boat.

An Egyptian Leader

Egypt is one of the most important countries in the Middle East. It is very old and has thousands of years of history. More Arabs (AIR-uhbz) live in Egypt than in the other countries in the Middle East. It is a powerful country, too. Egypt fought in five wars against Israel between 1948 and 1973.

In 1978, the Egyptian president was Anwar Sadat (AHN-whar suh-DOT). He took a big step. He decided it was time to make peace with Israel. U.S. President Jimmy Carter wanted to help.

Carter invited Sadat to Camp David in the United States. This is where presidents go on vacation. He also asked the prime minister of Israel, Menachem Begin (muh-NAW-kuhm BAY-ghin), to come. At first, the two leaders did not speak to each other directly. Carter had to go back and forth between them with messages. At last, they agreed to a peace treaty. It was called the Camp David Accords (uh-KORDZ).

Carter joins in as Sadat (left) shakes hands with Begin (right).

President Carter welcomes Anwar Sadat to the White House.

Anwar Sadat Pays a Price for Peace

The Camp David Accords was a huge event in the Middle East. Egypt was the first Arab country to make peace with Israel. The two leaders received the Nobel Peace Prize for their work. Still, not everyone was happy with these two leaders. In Egypt, there were many Islamic (iz-LAWM-ik) religious extremists. These people did not want any Arabs to make peace with Israel.

A few years later Sadat was watching a parade. One of the vehicles in the parade stopped right in front of him. Soldiers stepped out, shot and **assassinated** (uh-SAS-suh-nay-tuhd) Sadat. The shooters were Islamic extremists.

Anwar Sadat did a brave thing back in 1978. He saw that the Middle East needed peace. And he worked with his former enemy to bring about that peace.

Anwar Sadat speaks about the importance of peace in the Middle East.

Many Noble Accomplishments

Nobel prizes are awarded every year for many different categories. The categories include science, mathematics, peace, and economics. The awards ceremony is held in Stockholm, the capital of Sweden.

Before & After Sadat

In the early 1900s, Egypt was ruled by a king. In 1956, a man named Gamal Abdal Nasser (joo-MAHL AB-duhl NAH-suhr) led a **rebellion** that took the power away from the king. He was the first president of the Republic of Egypt. He was in office from 1956–1970.

After Sadat was killed, Muhammad Mubarak (moh-HAH-muhd moo-BAHR-uhk) took over as president. Some Egyptians feel that Mubarak ruled like a **dictator**. In 2005, several candidates ran for president in a general election. Mubarak won the presidency again.

Ayatollah Khomeini greets the crowd in Qom.

Not His First Name

The word *ayatollah* is not a name. It is a title given to religious leaders in Iran. It means "sign of God." Ayatollah Khomeini's first name was Ruhollah (ruh-HULL-uh).

Did You Know?

The people in Iran are not Arabs. Iranians are Persians (PUHR-zhuhnz). The official language of Iran is Farsi (FAR-see).

This is Iranian mail. The address is written in Farsi.

An Islamic Revolution in Iran

A **shah**, also known as a king, ruled Iran for many years. The United States liked this shah because he kept things stable. Stable leaders in the Middle East keep the price of oil low. Iran is a country very rich in oil. The shah became rich from the sale of this oil while his people remained poor. Many Iranians (ih-RAY-nee-uhnz) turned to their religious leaders for help. One religious leader in Iran was Ayatollah Khomeini (eye-uh-TOLL-uh ko-MAY-nee).

In 1979, the shah became sick with cancer. He left Iran to get medical help. After he left, an Islamic group took over Iran. They did not allow the shah to return to Iran. This group had started a **revolution** (rev-uh-LOO-shuhn). Khomeini became the leader of the country. He said that the Islamic religion would be the new law of the land.

Revolutionaries on a tank in Tehran

The American Hostage Crisis

In 1979, the people of Iran spoke out. They said they hated the United States. They did this because the United States had supported the shah. Some Iranians went to the American **embassy** (EM-buh-see). This embassy was in Tehran (tay-RAN), which is the capital of Iran. They broke into the embassy and took 90 American people as **hostages**. They released some of these hostages. But 52 people remained captive for more than a year.

President Jimmy Carter ordered a rescue mission. The helicopter sent to Iran crashed in the desert. Eight U.S. soldiers died in this crash. It was a hard time for Americans. But strangely, it united them, too.

On January 21, 1981, the Iranians let the hostages go. It was the same day Ronald Reagan became the next U.S. president. Unknown to the public, leaders of both countries had reached a secret deal. The United States sent guns to Iran for fighting. In return, Iran freed the hostages.

Reagan becomes the 40th president of the United States.

Nuclear power plant

The plane carrying the freed American hostages lands in Germany. The hostages were held in Iran for 444 days.

How Iran's Government Works

Iran's primary ruler is a religious figure. He is called the supreme leader. The Congress elects him. He is in command of the military and has more power than the other leaders who rule with him. Iran also has a president elected by the people. He serves as a spokesperson for the nation.

Nuclear Power

In recent times, Iran has been in the news because of nuclear power. Nuclear energy can be used for dangerous weapons. In 2006, the Iranian president told the world that Iran had a right to build nuclear weapons for protection. This made the Iranian people proud. But it alarmed the United States government.

Both the Dome of the Rock and the Wailing Wall are shown in this picture.

Who Controls Jerusalem?

Did you know that both Palestinians and Israelis consider Jerusalem their capital city? This argument is really about controlling this old city. Jerusalem has a special meaning for both groups of people. There are very important religious places there. When Arafat and the Israeli leaders began their peace talks, both sides would not agree to give up their stake on this city. Today, this is still an issue between Palestinians and Israelis.

Palestine's Struggle

The nation of Israel formed in 1948. Jewish people from around the world moved to Israel. This caused problems with those people who already lived in the region. The people who lived there before were Arab people. They were called Palestinians (pal-uh-STIN-ee-uhnz). Many Palestinians had to leave their homes. They became **refugees** (ref-you-JEEZ).

Yasir Arafat (YAH-sir AIR-uh-fat) was a Palestinian. He was born in 1929. After 1948, he struggled against Israel for many years. The Palestinians felt the Israelis (iz-RAY-leez) had taken their land. Arafat became the leader of the Palestine Liberation Organization, or PLO. The PLO led violent attacks against Israel. As a result, Israel treated the Palestinians poorly.

This image shows the Old City of Jerusalem.

Palestinian Uprising

In the 1970s and '80s, life became harder for the Palestinians. They lived in the West Bank and the Gaza Strip. These places were **occupied territories**. This means the Israeli army made all the rules and not the Palestinians.

In 1987, an uprising called the **intifada** (in-tuh-FAW-duh) began. The word *intifada* means "awakening." Many Palestinians were frustrated. Young people filled the streets. They threw rocks at the Israeli soldiers. They did this to show their anger about the occupation. The Palestinians looked to Arafat for leadership. He led this intifada.

In 1992, Israel elected a new prime minister. His name was Yitzhak Rabin (YIT-sock rah-BEAN). Tensions were heating up in Israel. Israelis hoped that this new leader would bring a change. Rabin had fought in many of the wars between Israel and its Arab neighbors. Now it was time to find peace with the Palestinians.

Palestinians throw rocks at Israeli soldiers.

Violence is a common occurrence in the Gaza Strip.

What's in a Nickname?

Did you know that Arafat had a nickname? He was called Abu Omar (AH-boo OH-mar). This means "The father of Omar." Many Arab men are given a similar nickname once they have a child.

How Palestine's Government Works

Palestinians elect their own president. He serves a four-year term. The president has many of the same powers as the president in the United States. But, the Palestinian president appoints a prime minister who handles the daily duties in the government. At any time, the president can remove the prime minister from office.

The First Palestinian President

Before Rabin, there had never been an Israeli leader who shook hands with Arafat. Rabin was the first to do that.

In 1993, Arafat and Rabin were able to reach an agreement. Secret meetings took place in Oslo (OZ-low), Norway. The agreement was called the Oslo Accords. It declared that the Palestinians could make their own rules and have their own rulers. In return, their attacks on Israel had to stop. Arafat agreed and became Palestine's first president.

Both Rabin and Arafat received the Nobel Peace Prize for this agreement. They were honored for their hard work toward peace in the Middle East.

Arafat adjusts his *kefiyyah* during a meeting.

Leading Israel

Golda Meir (meh-IR) worked in Israel's government for more than 25 years. In 1969, she became the prime minister. On October 6, 1973, the Yom Kippur (YOHM kip-POUR) War broke out. Israel was not prepared to fight this war. They were losing. Meir asked the United States for support. The United States helped turn the tide and the war ended.

In April 1974, Meir resigned as prime minister. Yitzhak Rabin was elected to take her place. Then, he was reelected in 1992.

Arafat's Hat

Arafat wore a head covering called a ***kefiyyah*** (kuh-FEE-yuh). It is a large, square piece of cloth that is folded and placed on the head. A thick rope kept the cloth in place.

Yitzhak Rabin visits a school during a peace demonstration. He hoped to bring peace to Israel and Palestine.

Rabin (left) and Arafat (right) share a historic handshake. President William Clinton stands between the two leaders.

Yitzhak Rabin Takes the First Steps Toward Peace

The Oslo Accords were a **compromise**. Both Israel and Palestine had to give in on certain things. Palestinians wanted to make their own rules. The Israelis wanted the Palestinians to stop attacking them. This sounded good to many people. But, there were still people who were not happy. Some Palestinians did not want to stop fighting against Israel. They still believed they should get their land back. Some Israelis did not like Rabin meeting with Arafat. They wanted the Palestinians to pay for the attacks on them. One of these Israelis was a Jewish religious extremist. He shot and assassinated Rabin in November 1995.

Both sides made some progress toward the Oslo Accords compromise. However, full peace between these two is still a future dream. The first steps toward peace began with Prime Minister Rabin. People who hope for peace in the Middle East still honor Rabin today.

Palestinians chant slogans to free Palestine.

Guards carry the coffin of Yitzhak Rabin.

Religious Extremists

Religious extremists can come from different religious backgrounds. In 1994, a Jewish extremist killed many Muslims as they prayed on a religious holiday. Osama bin Laden and the 19 men who attacked the United States on September 11, 2001, are examples of Islamic extremists.

Palestinian Women

In some Palestinian homes, parents choose whom their daughters and sons will marry. Sometimes, women are forced to marry men who are many years older. But times are changing for Palestinian women. In 2005, the first Palestinian woman was elected mayor in her small town on the West Bank. More women are being elected to Parliament, too. Now, they are beginning to make decisions about schools and jobs.

Hussein's Hero

Before the 1950s, Egypt was part of the British empire. The British controlled the trade routes that led through Egypt. The British had control over Egypt's king, too. Many people did not like this king. When Hussein was just a teenager, a man named Gamal Abdal Nasser defeated the British-controlled king in Egypt. Nasser took over and became Egypt's president. It was the first time in 2,000 years that Egyptians controlled Egypt. This event made Nasser a hero to Hussein.

Jordan's Leader

For almost 50 years, Jordan was led by King Hussein. Though they shared the same name, there was no relation between King Hussein and Saddam Hussein of Iraq. King Hussein worked for peace between Jordan and Israel. This was finally accomplished in 1994.

Saddam Hussein

Oil in the Middle East

About 65 percent of the oil in the world is in the Middle East. Much of this oil is in the country of Iraq. Only Saudi Arabia has more. The Middle East works together to control the price of oil. At one time, they limited the amount of oil they sent to the United States. They were angry that the United States helped Israel.

Nations all around the world depend on oil. Gas for automobiles comes from oil. Oil makes electricity and heats homes, too. Conflicts in the Middle East cause oil prices to rise. They affect anyone who depends on oil. This is one reason the world pays close attention to the Middle East.

From 1979 to 2003, Saddam Hussein ruled Iraq. He was a violent and cruel leader. Hussein was not afraid to start wars with those around him. He was also involved in two wars with the United States. One of these wars had to do with his desire to have more oil.

Much of the oil produced in the Middle East is used for transportation.

Saddam Hussein Against the World

In 1990, Hussein wanted to control a small country named Kuwait (koo-WAYT). This country borders Iraq and it produces lots of oil. In fact, it has almost as much oil as Iraq.

Hussein wanted to take control of Kuwait's oil to make himself richer. The United Nations knew what Hussein was planning to do. They warned him to not attack Kuwait. U.S. President George H. W. Bush led a group of nations against Hussein. These nations sent warships and tanks to Kuwait. In just a few days, Hussein's army was defeated. He left Kuwait, but he did not leave quietly. His army set oil wells on fire and tried to destroy what they could. This is called the Persian Gulf War.

Because of this war, he had to allow UN inspectors into his country. These inspectors kept a watchful eye on Hussein. They needed to make sure he was not planning any more attacks.

These oil wells in Kuwait were set on fire by Hussein's army.

President George H. W. Bush

President George W. Bush

Father and Son Presidents

The 41st president of the United States was George H. W. Bush. He is the father of the 43rd president, George W. Bush. Both of these presidents fought wars against Saddam Hussein.

Hussein and Stalin

Some people think that Hussein was a lot like Joseph Stalin, a ruler from Communist Russia. Hussein not only looked like Stalin, but his actions as a leader were very similar, too. In an interview, Hussein's biographer said that Hussein's personal library was full of books on Stalin.

In April 2003, U.S. forces captured Baghdad. Iraqis soon tore down this large statue of Hussein.

What Did They Find?

No one has found nuclear weapons in Iraq. Some people wonder if a war should have been started. Others think it was worth it to remove such a terrible leader.

Land of Many Peoples

Iraq consists of many different people. There are two major Islamic groups, the Sunnis (SOO-neez) and the Shiites (SHE-eyetz). There are also Kurdish (KUR-dish) people in the north, who have a very different culture from their Arab countrymen.

Hussein's Last Stand

In 2003, people were afraid that Hussein was up to no good. He had kicked out the UN inspectors. No one could check up on him to see what he was planning. Some world leaders believed Iraq was making powerful **nuclear** (NOO-klee-uhr) **weapons**. No one wanted a man like Hussein to have weapons like these.

President George W. Bush led other nations to join in an attack on Iraq. At first, everyone thought the war would end quickly. Troops captured Baghdad (BAG-dad), the capital of Iraq. On December 13, 2003, they captured Hussein hiding in a **bunker**. Iraqis (ih-ROCK-eez) put him on trial. They convicted him of crimes against humanity and hanged him.

As of 2007, troops were still in Iraq. No one is sure how long they will stay. They are fighting **insurgents** (in-SURG-uhntz) from Islamic nations. These insurgents want to keep Iraq from forming a new set of laws. But most Iraqis want to live in peace.

Many people believed Hussein was hiding nuclear weapons in Iraq. None have been found.

Will There Ever Be Peace?

The Middle East is a hard place to understand. Much of it is a story of conflict and violence. Some conflicts come from religious extremism. Israel is often in the middle of conflicts there. Plus, the world needs a lot of oil. Because the Middle East has so much oil, problems often happen there.

However, there are bright moments of peace in the Middle East. Some courageous leaders have found the strength to work for peace. They know that those who do not want peace might assassinate them. But these leaders take these risks for the good of the Middle East. It is their hope that there will be a day when peace is more common than conflict.

The Middle East has beautiful cities and landscapes. They are often overshadowed by all the wars and violence.

The Euphrates River is an important source of water for the Middle East.

Queen Noor

Religion in the Middle East

In the Middle East, most Arab people are Muslims (MUHZ-luhmz). Their religion is called Islam. There are also many different Christians in the region. Judaism (JOO-dee-izuhm) is another major religion.

Helping Others Understand

Elizabeth Halaby was born in Washington, D.C. She worked for the royal airline in Jordan. That is where she met King Hussein. She married the king and converted to Islam. She also changed her name to Noor al-Hussein. She has served as an expert advisor to the United Nations. Queen Noor gives speeches about understanding the Middle East. She has spent her life working toward improving life in the Middle East.

Glossary

assassinated—murdered by surprise attack; usually a prominent person for political reasons

bunker—an underground hideout that keeps someone safe from attacks

compromise—an agreement in which each side must give in a little

conflict—a fight, battle, or war between people or groups of people

dictator—a single ruler of a country who has complete control

embassy—a location within a country's capital where the representative of a foreign country lives

hostages—people who are captured and held in order for the hostage taker to get something he or she wants

insurgents—those who fight in an area against the people in charge

intifada—an Arabic word meaning "awakening"; refers to the Palestinian uprising from 1987–1993 against Israel's occupation

kefiyyah—a head-dress worn by many Arab men

nuclear weapons—bombs and missiles that explode with great force

occupied territories—Palestinian areas occupied by the Israeli army: West Bank and Gaza Strip

rebellion—a fight against the leaders

refugees—people who are forced to flee their homes and must live somewhere else

religious extremism—the use of religious beliefs to justify violence against other people

revolution—a change in a nation's government without an election

shah—an Iranian word for king

Index

Image Credits

cover Time & Life Pictures/Getty Images; p.1 Time & Life Pictures/Getty Images; p.4 Jacques Langevin/Corbis Sygma; p.5 Scott Rothstein/Shutterstock, Inc.; p.6 (top) zju/Shutterstock, Inc.; p.6 (bottom) Adrian Beesley/istockphoto.com; p.7 David Rubinger/Time & Life Pictures/Getty Images; p.8 Library of Congress; p.9 (top) Courtesy of the Nobel Committee; p.9 (bottom) Bettmann/Corbis; p.10 (top) Patrick Chauvel/Sygma/Corbis; p.10 (bottom) phy/Shutterstock, Inc.; p.11 Michel Setboun/Corbis; p.12 Jean Louis Atlan/Sygma/Corbis; p.13 (top) Bettmann/Corbis; p.13 (bottom) Photos.com; p.14 Boris Katsman/Shutterstock, Inc.; p.15 Photos.com; p.16 Peter Turnley/Corbis; p.17 AFP/Getty Images; p.18 Thomas Hartwell/ Corbis; p.19 (top) David Rubinger/ Corbis; p.19 (bottom) Reuters/Corbis; p.20 Loay Abu Haykel/Reuters/Corbis; p.21 AFP/Getty Images; p.22 Jacques Pavlovsky/Sygma/Corbis; p.23 Photos.com; p.24 Peter Turnley/Corbis; p.25 (top) U.S. Senate; p.25 (bottom) U.S. Senate; p.26 AFP/Getty Images;
p.27 John Wollwerth/Shutterstock, Inc.; p.28 Yehuda Boltshauser/Shutterstock, Inc.;
p.29 (top) Photos.com; p.29 (bottom) Mehdi Fedouach/AFP/Getty Images